Rhythm Work

Level Three

By Wesley Schaum

Schaum's Pathway to Musicianship

The *Schaum Making Music Piano Library* integrates method, theory, technic and note reading with appealing materials for recital and repertoire. Schaum's well-proven motivational philosophy and sound pedagogy are widely recognized.

FOREWORD

The purpose of this book is to help develop an understanding and feeling for the fundamental rhythms in music. It is intended as a supplement for any Level Three method book and for students of <u>all ages</u>.

It is intended that all lessons with music notation be <u>played at the keyboard</u>, in addition to the written work. In this way, the student gets a <u>feeling</u> for the various rhythms plus valuable rhythmic reading experience.

INDEX

Schaum Publications, Inc.

EXCLUSIVELY DISTRIBUTED BY

HAL•LEONARD®
CORPORATION

7777 W. BLUEMOUND RD. P.O. BOX 13819 MILWAUKEE, WI 53213

Lesson 1. Review of 16th Notes in 2/4, 3/4 and 4/4

Name _____   Date _____   Score _____

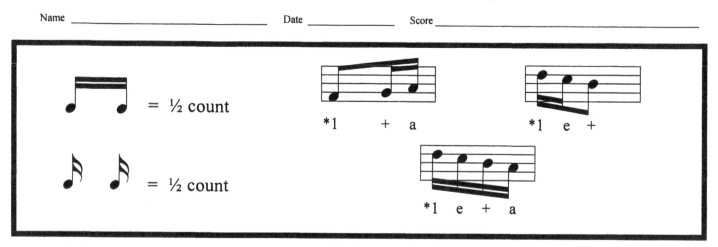

DIRECTIONS: Write in the counting for each measure. Be sure that the numbers and abbreviations are carefully placed *directly below* the note or rest to which they apply.

(Write the counting numbers for each measure.)

KEYBOARD ASSIGNMENT: After writing in the counting above, all lines of music should be *played at the keyboard.* [Optional:] Count aloud as you play.

*TEACHER'S NOTE: The subdivided counts are to be said, "one - ee - and - ah," etc. The plus sign (+) is the abbreviation for "and." You may prefer other ways of counting the subdivided beats. Four syllable words such as "Mis-sis-sip-pi" or "Chat-ta-noo-ga" may also be used.

Lesson 2. Review of 16th Notes in 3/8 and 6/8

Name _____ Date _____ Score _____

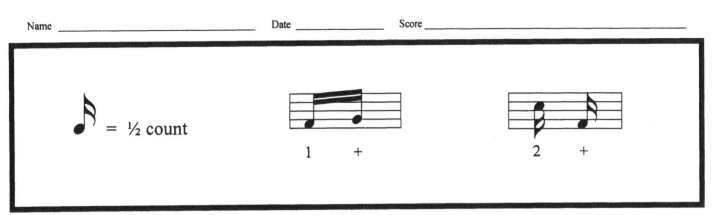

DIRECTIONS: Write in the counting for each measure. Be sure that the numbers and abbreviations are carefully placed *directly below* the note or rest to which they apply.

1   2   3   +

(sample)

KEYBOARD ASSIGNMENT: After writing in the counting above, all lines of music should be *played at the keyboard.* [Optional:] Count aloud as you play.

Name _____ Date _____ Score _____

TEMPO *(TEM-po)* is the rate of speed at which music is played.
Tempos may be divided into three basic groups:

SLOW TEMPOS
Largo *(LAHR-goh)* Very slow.
Larghetto *(lahr-GET-oh)* A little faster than Largo.
Lento *(LEN-toh)* Slow.
Adagio *(ah-DAH-jee-oh)* Slow; a little slower than Andante.

MEDIUM TEMPOS
Andante *(ahn-DAHN-tay)* Medium slow; at the speed of a medium walk.
Andantino *(ahn-dahn-TEE-noh)* A little faster than Andante.
Moderato *(mod-dur-AH-toh)* Medium speed.

FAST TEMPOS
Allegretto *(ah-leh-GRET-toh)* Less fast than Allegro.
Allegro *(ah-LEG-grow)* Fast.
Vivace *(vee-VAH-chay)* Quickly.
Presto *(PRESS-toh)* Very Fast.

DIRECTIONS: Below are many different tempos mixed together.
Write the letter "S," "M," or "F" on the dotted line next to each tempo.

    S = Slow   **M = Medium**   **F = Fast**

Andantino ....   **Andante**.....................   **Allegro** ....

Moderato ....   **Largo** ....   **Lento** ....

Presto ....   **Allegretto**..................   **Adagio** ....

Larghetto ....   **Vivace** ....   **Andantino** ....

Lesson 4. Tempo Marks: Slowest and Fastest

Name _____ Date _____ Score _____

DIRECTIONS: Draw a circle around the *slower* tempo in each pair.

Presto – Largo   Allegro – Adagio

Moderato – Vivace   Andante – Moderato

Andantino – Lento   Vivace – Allegretto

Larghetto – Presto   Largo – Andantino

Allegretto – Moderato   Lento – Allegro

DIRECTIONS: Draw a circle around the *faster* tempo in each pair.

Largo – Vivace   Presto – Moderato

Allegro – Presto   Andante – Larghetto

Lento – Allegro   Allegretto – Largo

Moderato – Allegretto   Andante – Vivace

Andantino – Larghetto   Adagio – Lento

DIRECTIONS: Draw a circle around the *slowest* tempo in each group.

Larghetto – Largo – Presto   Lento – Andante – Andantino

Lento – Andante – Vivace   Allegro – Allegretto – Presto

Adagio – Moderato – Andante   Largo – Vivace – Moderato

Andante – Andantino – Allegro   Presto – Vivace – Allegretto

Lesson 5. Tempo Marks: Style and Mood

Name _____ Date _____ Score _____

When playing the piano, you often must pretend that you are an "actor" in a theater – showing in your playing, different feelings and moods to your "audience". These tempo marks explain the mood or "feeling" to be shown while playing the music.

Animato *(an-nee-MAH-toh)* Lively, with spirit.

Cantabile *(cahn-TAH-bil-lay)* In a smooth, singing style.

Dolce *(DOLE-chay)* Sweetly, gently.

Espressivo *(ess-press-SEE-voh)* With expression.

Giocoso *(jee-oh-KOH-soh)* Playfully, full of fun.

Grazioso *(gra-tsee-OH-soh)* Gracefully.

Leggiero *(led-jee-AIR-oh)* Lightly, delicately.

Maestoso *(my-ess-TOH-soh)* Majestic, proudly.

Misterioso *(miss-teer-ee-OH-soh)* Mysteriously, spooky.

Semplice *(SEMM-plee-chay)* Simple, plain.

Vivo *(VEE-voh)* Full of life and energy.

DIRECTIONS: Draw a circle around the tempo mark which correctly matches the description.

Lightly, delicately .... **Maestoso – Giocoso – Leggiero**

Simple, plain .... **Vivo – Semplice – Dolce**

Lively, with spirit.. **Animato – Grazioso – Misterioso**

With expression... **Cantabile – Dolce – Espressivo**

Playfully, full of fun.................................... **Leggiero – Vivo – Giocoso**

Mysteriously, spooky .... **Maestoso – Misterioso – Semplice**

Gracefully .... **Grazioso – Espressivo – Cantabile**

TEACHER'S NOTE: The tempo marks shown on this page are commonly found at Level 3. There are, of course, many other musical terms which the student should learn eventually. Schaum method books include a short dictionary at the back of each book, listing additional terms.

Lesson 6. Tempo Marks: Defining Style and Mood

Name _____ Date _____ Score _____

DIRECTIONS: Draw a circle around the correct definition for each tempo mark.

Cantabile ....In a smooth, singing style. – Lightly, delicately.

Animato ....Full of life and energy. – Lively, with spirit.

Dolce ....Simple, plain. – Sweetly, gently.

Espressivo ....Gracefully. – With expression.

Giocoso ....Playfully, full of fun. – Majestic, proudly.

Vivo ....Mysteriously, spooky. – Full of life and energy.

Semplice ....With expression. – Simple, plain.

Leggiero ....Lightly, delicately. – Sweetly, gently.

Maestoso ....Majestic, proudly. – Lively, with spirit.

Giocoso ....Full of life and energy. – Playfully, full of fun.

Grazioso ....Gracefully. – Sweetly, gently.

Misterioso ....Mysteriously, spooky. – In a smooth, singing style.

Animato ....Playfully, full of fun. – Lively, with spirit.

Espressivo ....Simple, plain. – With expression.

Cantabile ....In a smooth, singing style. – Gracefully.

Dolce ....Sweetly, gently. – Majestic, proudly.

Vivo ....Full of life and energy. – Lightly, delicately.

Semplice ....Lively, with spirit. – Simple, plain.

Lesson 7. Review of Staccato and Extension Dots

Name _____   Date _____   Score _____

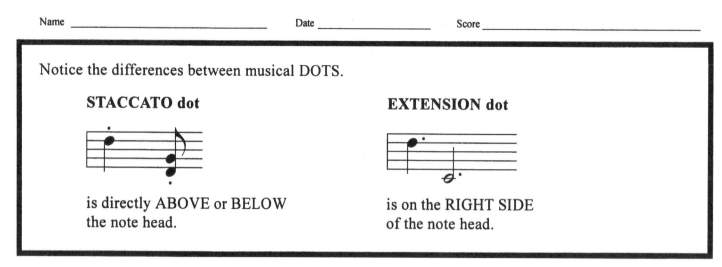

Notice the differences between musical DOTS.

STACCATO dot

is directly ABOVE or BELOW
the note head.

EXTENSION dot

is on the RIGHT SIDE
of the note head.

*DIRECTIONS: Draw a *red* circle around all STACCATO dots.
Draw a *green* circle around all EXTENSION dots.

Circle the correct answer:

Does the *staccato dot* change the counting of the note value?   **yes** / **no**

Does the *dot on the right side* of the note change the counting of the note value?   **yes** / **no**

*TEACHER'S NOTE: Crayon, ball-point pen or colored pencil may be used by the student. If the specified color is not available, the teacher may designate a substitute. Dotted rests are explained in Lesson 28.

Lesson 8. Review of Ties and Slurs

Name _____ Date _____ Score _____

DIRECTIONS: On the dotted lines, write the word "TIE" or "SLUR" next to each arrow, depending upon where the arrow is pointing (see sample).

(sample)

(Write the word "TIE" or "SLUR")

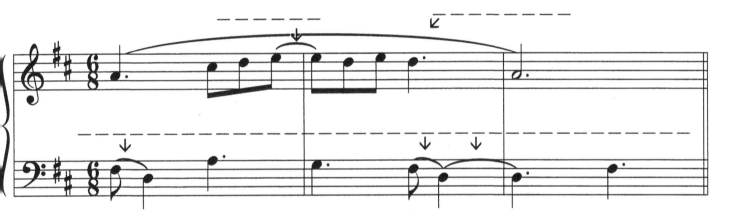

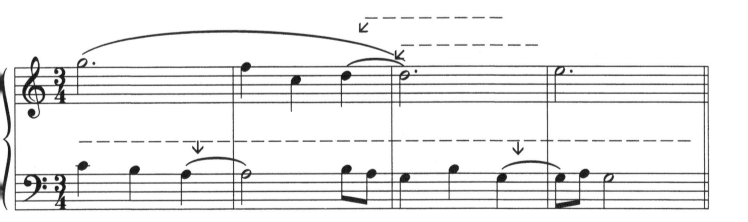

Circle the correct answer:

Does a TIE change the length of any note values? **yes** / **no**

Does a SLUR change the length of any note values? **yes** / **no**

KEYBOARD ASSIGNMENT: After completing the written work, play each line of music, *hands separately* (right hand alone, then left hand alone.) If necessary, count aloud as you play. Be aware of the differences between ties and slurs as you play.

Lesson 9.   Syncopated Rhythm: (8th-Quarter-8th)

Name _____   Date _____   Score _____

Syncopation is a kind of rhythm with emphasis on a weak beat or between beats. One very common syncopation is the 8th-quarter-8th pattern. In the sample line below, the syncopated patterns are indicated with a *horizontal bracket above the staff*. The syncopated beats are *circled*. Syncopated rhythms are often found in ragtime, jazz and most forms of popular music.

DIRECTIONS: Draw a bracket above each 8th-quarter-8th pattern. Watch for different time signatures. Write the counting numbers on the dotted line below each measure. Then draw a circle around each syncopated beat. Be sure to do the Keyboard Assignment, below.

KEYBOARD ASSIGNMENT: After completing the written work, play all notes at the keyboard three times per day. Be aware of the syncopated patterns. [Optional] Count aloud as you play.

Lesson 10. Syncopated Patterns in 2/4 and 3/4

Name _____ Date _____ Score _____

In the sample lines below, the syncopated patterns are indicated with a *horizontal bracket above the staff.* The syncopated beats are *circled.*

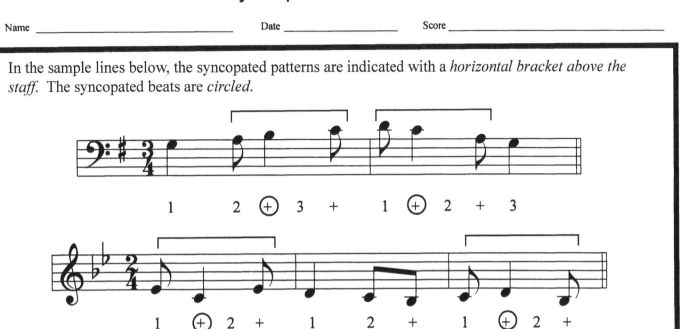

DIRECTIONS: Draw a bracket above each 8th-quarter-8th syncopated pattern (see Lesson 9). Watch for different time signatures. Write the counting numbers on the dotted line below each measure. Then circle the beats where the syncopated notes occur. Be sure to do the Keyboard Assignment, below.

KEYBOARD ASSIGNMENT: After completing the written work, play all notes at the keyboard three times per day. Be aware of the syncopated patterns. [Optional] Count aloud as you play.

Lesson 11. Eighth Note Triplets

Name _____ Date _____ Score _____

A TRIPLET is a group of three notes played in the usual time of two similar notes. A triplet is usually indicated with a slur or bracket and the number 3. The slur or bracket may appear above or below the notes of the triplet.

DIRECTIONS: Write in the counting on the dotted lines for every measure (see sample).

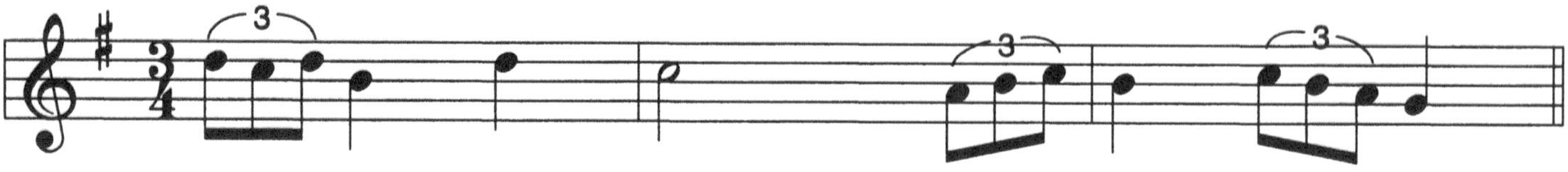

1 * * 2   3

(Choose and write in a method of counting.)

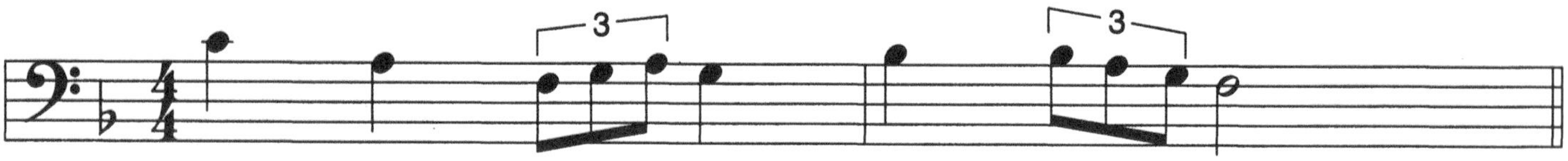

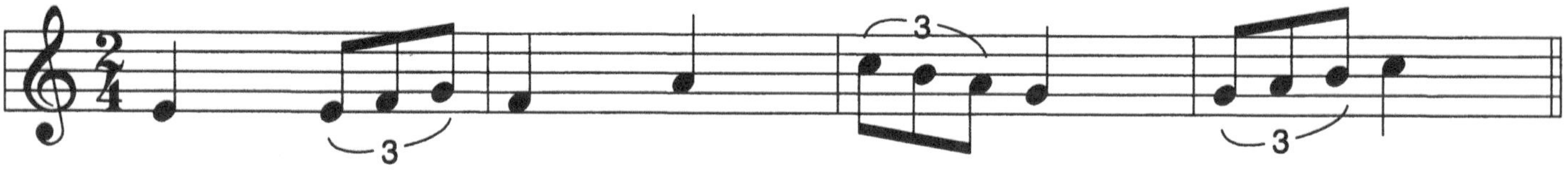

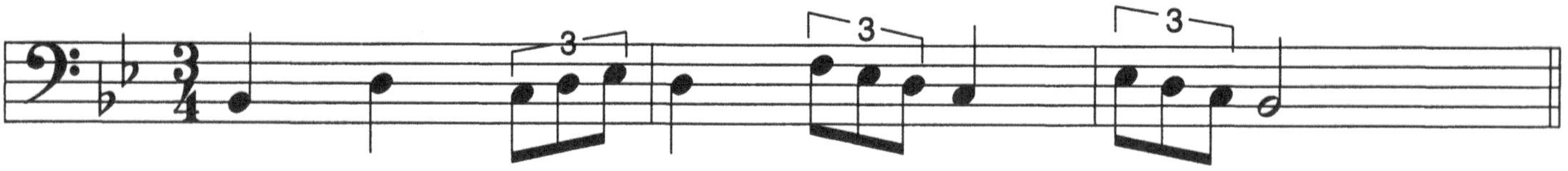

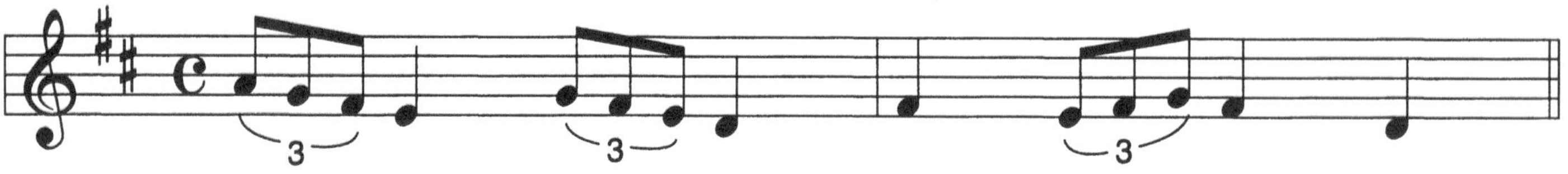

KEYBOARD ASSIGNMENT: After finishing the written work on this page, all lines of music should be *played at the keyboard*. The first note of each triplet should receive a slight accent.

*TEACHER'S NOTE: Because of different ways of teaching, the counting of triplet groups has purposely been left to the preference of the teacher. As a suggestion, you could use: "one-lah-lee," "two-lah-lee," etc. (the spoken number, of course, would depend upon the number of the beat). Three-syllable words, such as: "trip-oh-let," "choc-oh-let," and "beau-ti-ful" are other possibilities.

Lesson 12. Triplets in Various Time Signatures

Name _____   Date _____   Score _____

DIRECTIONS: On the staffs below, some of the measure bar lines are missing. Write in the counting on the dotted lines (watch for *different time signatures*). Then draw in bar lines where necessary to make the proper number of counts in each measure.

(Write in the counting.)

(Write in the counting, then draw in the bar lines.)

KEYBOARD ASSIGNMENT: After finishing the written work on this page, all lines of music should be *played at the keyboard*. The first note of each triplet should receive a *slight* accent.

Lesson 13. Additional Triplets

Name _____ Date _____ Score _____

DIRECTIONS: On the staffs below, some of the measure bar lines are missing. Write in the counting on the dotted lines (watch for *different time signatures*). Then draw in bar lines where necessary to make the proper number of counts in each measure.

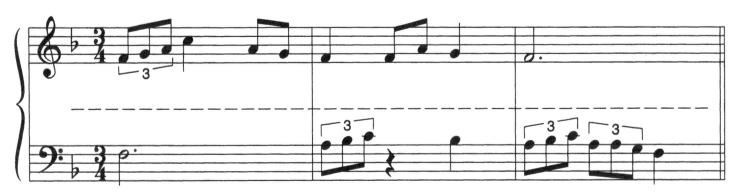

(Write in the counting, then draw in the bar lines.)

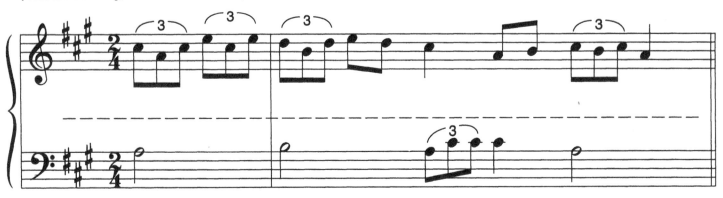

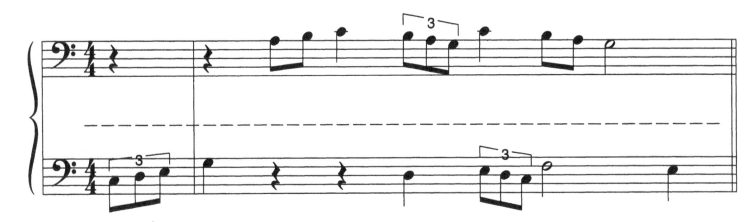

KEYBOARD ASSIGNMENT: After finishing the written work on this page, all lines of music should be *played at the keyboard*. The first note of each triplet should receive a *slight* accent.

Lesson 14.   Rhythm Quiz No. 1

Name _____ Date _____ Score _____

DIRECTIONS: Match each musical sign with its description by placing the corresponding alphabetical letter on the line beside the description.

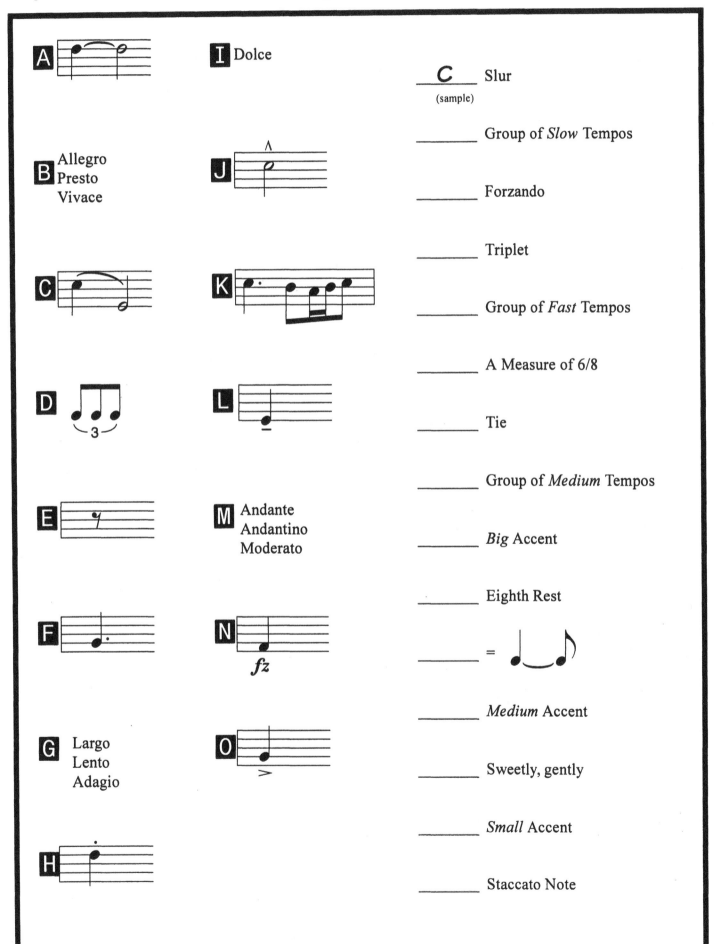

_C_ Slur
(sample)

_____ Group of *Slow* Tempos

_____ Forzando

_____ Triplet

_____ Group of *Fast* Tempos

_____ A Measure of 6/8

_____ Tie

_____ Group of *Medium* Tempos

_____ *Big* Accent

_____ Eighth Rest

_____ =

_____ *Medium* Accent

_____ Sweetly, gently

_____ *Small* Accent

_____ Staccato Note

Lesson 15. Divided Accompaniment

Name _____ Date _____ Score _____

In a DIVIDED ACCOMPANIMENT one hand plays the melody notes while the other hand plays the accompaniment notes BELOW and ABOVE (crossing over) the melody.

DIVIDED ACCOMPANIMENT is counted the same as a regular accompaniment.

DIRECTIONS: Write in the counting (on the dotted lines provided) ONLY for the *divided accompaniment* in each measure.

(sample)

(Write in the counting.)

KEYBOARD ASSIGNMENT: After finishing the written work on this page, all lines of music should be played at the keyboard. The hand playing the accompaniment will have to cross over to play some of the notes.

Lesson 16. More Divided Accompaniment

Name _____   Date _____   Score _____

DIRECTIONS: Write in the counting (on the dotted lines provided) ONLY for the *divided accompaniment* in each measure.

(Write in the counting.)

KEYBOARD ASSIGNMENT: After finishing the written work on this page, all lines of music should be played at the keyboard. The hand playing the accompaniment will have to cross over to play some of the notes.

Lesson 17. Melody Divided Between Hands

A DIVIDED MELODY occurs when the melody notes are written on two staffs and are played with two hands.

A divided melody is counted the same as a group of notes written on one staff.

Divided melody notes may be written:

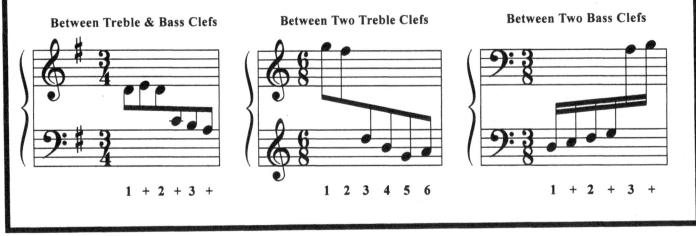

DIRECTIONS: Write in the counting (on the dotted lines provided) ONLY for the *divided melody* as it appears in different measures.

Lesson 18. Hold or Fermata

Name _____ Date _____ Score _____

A "HOLD" or FERMATA (⌒) allows the performer to interrupt the regular counting and "hold" some of the notes longer than usual.

* Notes directly below a "Hold" sign are usually held for about 1 to 3 extra beats. The letter "H" is used in this book to show where extra beats are added for the "held" notes. The "Hold" sign is used in different ways:

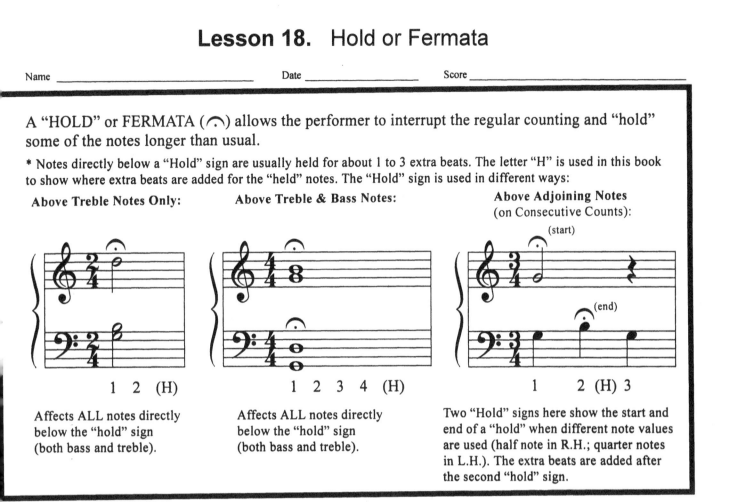

Above Treble Notes Only:

1   2   (H)

Affects ALL notes directly below the "hold" sign (both bass and treble).

Above Treble & Bass Notes:

1   2   3   4   (H)

Affects ALL notes directly below the "hold" sign (both bass and treble).

Above Adjoining Notes (on Consecutive Counts):

(start)

(end)

1   2 (H) 3

Two "Hold" signs here show the start and end of a "hold" when different note values are used (half note in R.H.; quarter notes in L.H.). The extra beats are added after the second "hold" sign.

DIRECTIONS: Draw a circle around each "HOLD" symbol. Then write in the counting for each measure. Write the letter "H" to show where the extra beats are to be added (see sample).

(sample)   **1   2   3   (H)**

(Write in "H" for hold.)

*TEACHER'S NOTE: At first, it is recommended that the "hold" be taught as having specific extra beats. The counting of these additional beats is left to the preference of the teacher. As a suggestion, a quarter-note with a hold could be counted: "one-pause-hold" or "one-wait-wait." Of course, as the student gains more experience, he should develop a "feeling" for the length of the hold and eventually abandon the system of specific extra beats.

Lesson 19. Dotted Eighth and Sixteenth

Name _____   Date _____   Score _____

A DOTTED EIGHTH note is equal to one EIGHTH note tied to one SIXTEENTH note.

*1 + a 2   3 + a 4

*DIRECTIONS: On the staffs below, some of the measure bar lines are missing. Write in the counting on the dotted lines. Then draw in bar lines where necessary to make the proper number of counts in each measure.

(Choose and write in a method of counting.)

(Write in the counting, then draw in the bar lines.)

KEYBOARD ASSIGNMENT: After finishing the written work on this page, all lines of music should be *played at the keyboard.*

*TEACHER'S NOTE: The counting here is derived from the counting of four successive 16th notes, explained in Lesson 1. The counting, 1 + a 2, is to be spoken "one - and - ah - two." (*Ah* represents the 16th note.) The spoken numbers, of course, would depend upon the numbers of the beats. If you prefer, a different type of counting may be used. The "Star Spangled Banner" is an excellent piece to illustrate the dotted 8th and 16th rhythm.

Lesson 20. Dotted 8th and 16th in Various Time Signatures

Name _____   Date _____   Score _____

DIRECTIONS: On the staffs below, some of the measure bar lines are missing. Write in the counting on the dotted lines (watch for *different time signatures*). Then draw in bar lines where necessary to make the proper number of counts in each measure.

1   +   a   2

(sample)

(Write in the counting, similar to Lesson 19.)

(Write in the counting, then draw in the bar lines.)

KEYBOARD ASSIGNMENT: After finishing the written work on this page, all lines of music should be *played at the keyboard*. [Optional] Count aloud as you play.

Lesson 21. Additional dotted 8th and 16ths

Name _____ Date _____ Score _____

DIRECTIONS: On the staffs below, some of the measure bar lines are missing. Write in the counting on the dotted lines (watch for *different time signatures*). Then draw in bar lines where necessary to make the proper number of counts in each measure.

(Write in the counting.)

(Write in the counting, then draw in the bar lines.)

KEYBOARD ASSIGNMENT: After finishing the written work on this page, all lines of music should be *played at the keyboard.* [Optional:] Count aloud as you play.

Lesson 22. Rolled Chords

Name _____   Date _____   Score _____

*ROLLED CHORDS (Broken Chords) have a waved line (⸿) placed before an interval or chord.
The notes are played in rapid succession, usually from the lowest note upwards. Rolled chords do
not affect the counting.

as written: as played: as written: as played:

DIRECTIONS: Draw a circle around the ROLLED CHORDS. Then write in the counting on the
dotted lines.

KEYBOARD ASSIGNMENT: After finishing the written work on this page, all lines of music
should be *played at the keyboard.* [Optional:] Count aloud as you play.

*TEACHER'S NOTE: The *rolled chord* is sometimes called an *arpeggiated chord.*

Lesson 23.   Syncopated Rhythm: 8th-Dotted-Quarter

Name _____   Date _____   Score _____

Another common syncopation is the 8th-dotted-quarter pattern. In the sample line below, this syncopated pattern is indicated with a *horizontal bracket above the staff.* The syncopated beats are *circled.*

DIRECTIONS: Draw a bracket above each 8th-dotted-quarter pattern. Watch for different time signatures. Write the counting numbers on the dotted line below each measure. Then circle the beats where the syncopated notes occur. Be sure to do the Keyboard Assignment, below.

KEYBOARD ASSIGNMENT: After completing the written work, play all notes at the keyboard three times per day. [Optional] Count aloud as you play.

Lesson 24. Review of Syncopated Patterns

Name _____   Date _____   Score _____

Two common syncopated patterns are shown here. For examples of counting, see Lessons 9 and 23.

DIRECTIONS: Draw a bracket above each syncopated pattern, as shown above. Watch for different time signatures. Write the counting numbers on the dotted line below each measure. Then circle the beats where the syncopated notes occur. Be sure to do the Keyboard Assignment, below.

(sample)

KEYBOARD ASSIGNMENT: After completing the written work, play all notes at the keyboard three times per day. [Optional] Count aloud as you play.

For *additional syncopation study*, use the Schaum SYNCOPATION WORKBOOK (Catalog #02-20).

Lesson 25. "Cut Time" (2/2 Time)

Name _____   Date _____   Score _____

New Time Signatures:

2/2 Time and "CUT TIME" (¢) are counted the same.
Cut Time is sometimes called "ALLA BREVE" *(al-la BREV).*

DIRECTIONS: On the staffs below, some of the measure bar lines are missing. Write in the counting on the dotted lines. Then draw in bar lines where necessary to make the proper number of counts in each measure.

KEYBOARD ASSIGNMENT: After finishing the written work on this page, all lines of music should be *played at the keyboard.* [Optional] Count aloud as you play.

Lesson 26. Dotted Half Notes in "Cut Time"

Name _____ Date _____ Score _____

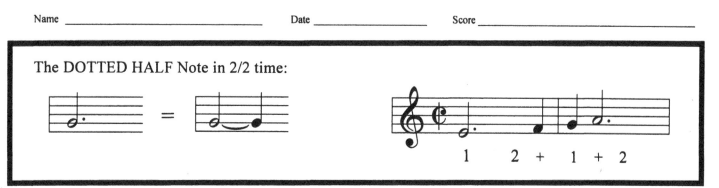

The DOTTED HALF Note in 2/2 time:

1   2 +   1 + 2

DIRECTIONS: On the staffs below, some of the measure bar lines are missing. Write in the counting on the dotted lines. Then draw in bar lines where necessary to make the proper number of counts in each measure.

(Write in the counting.)

(Write in the counting, then draw in the bar lines.)

KEYBOARD ASSIGNMENT: After finishing the written work on this page, all lines of music should be *played at the keyboard.* [Optional] Count aloud as you play.

Lesson 27. 9/8 Time Signature

Name _____ Date _____ Score _____

NEW Time Signature

Upper Number means
9 Counts per measure.

Lower Number means
EIGHTH NOTE gets
One Count.

= 1 count   = 2 counts

= 1 count   = 3 counts   = 6 counts

DIRECTIONS: On the staffs below, some of the measure bar lines are missing. Write in the counting on the dotted lines. Then draw in bar lines where necessary to make the proper number of counts in each measure.

(sample) 1 2 3 4 5 6 7 8 9

(Write in the counting.)

(Write in the counting, then draw in the bar lines.)

KEYBOARD ASSIGNMENT: After finishing the written work on this page, all lines of music should be *played at the keyboard.* [Optional] Count aloud as you play.

Lesson 28.   Dotted Rests

Name _____   Date _____   Score _____

DOTTED RESTS are counted the same as dotted notes.

DIRECTIONS: On the staffs below, some of the measure bar lines are missing. Write in the counting on the dotted lines. Then draw in bar lines where necessary to make the proper number of counts in each measure.

(Write in the counting, then draw in the bar lines.)

(Draw in the proper rest to complete each measure – use a dotted rest where possible.)

KEYBOARD ASSIGNMENT: After completing the written work, play all notes at the keyboard three times per day. [Optional] Count aloud as you play.

Lesson 29.   Trills

Name _____   Date _____   Score _____

*The TRILL (*tr⌁*) is a musical ornament that is produced by rapidly alternating the principal note with the next *scale note* above. The *principal note* is the note below the trill symbol. The principal note and the upper trill note are both affected by key signatures and accidentals.

The combined length of all notes in a trill must be the same as the length of the principal note. For example, if the principal note is a quarter note, the trill will consist of four 16th notes.

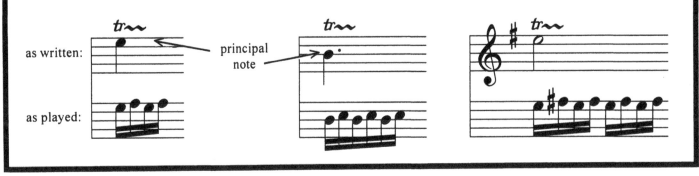

DIRECTIONS: Draw a *circle* around each TRILL symbol and principal note. Then write out the notes that should be played for each trill, using the blank staff below each measure. Add an accidental to the upper trill note if it is affected by the key signature.

KEYBOARD ASSIGNMENT: After finishing the written work on this page, play each trill *at the keyboard.*

*TEACHER'S NOTE: It is recommended that the student's first encounter be with a basic "measured" trill (equivalent to 16th notes) starting on the principal note. Trills beginning on the upper note, as well as "improvised" or "free-style" trills may be presented at a later time.

Lesson 30. Time Signature Review

Name _____   Date _____   Score _____

DIRECTIONS: On the staffs below, some of the measure bar lines are missing. Write in the counting on the dotted lines (watch for *different time signatures*). Then draw in bar lines where necessary to make the proper number of counts in each measure.

(Write in the counting, then draw in the bar lines.)

DIRECTIONS: Draw a CIRCLE around the correct answers.

C is counted the same as: 2/2   2/4   3/4   4/4

¢ is counted the same as: 2/2   2/4   3/4   4/4

In 4/4 time, what kind of note gets ONE count: 𝅝   𝅗𝅥   ♩   ♪

In 6/8 time, what kind of note gets ONE count: 𝅝   𝅗𝅥   ♩   ♪

In 2/2 time, what kind of note gets ONE count: 𝅝   𝅗𝅥   ♩   ♪

KEYBOARD ASSIGNMENT: After finishing the written work on this page, all lines of music should be *played at the keyboard.* [Optional:] Count aloud as you play.

Lesson 31. Rhythm Quiz No. 2

Name _____ Date _____ Score _____

DIRECTIONS: Match each musical sign with its description by placing the corresponding alphabetical letter on the line beside the description.

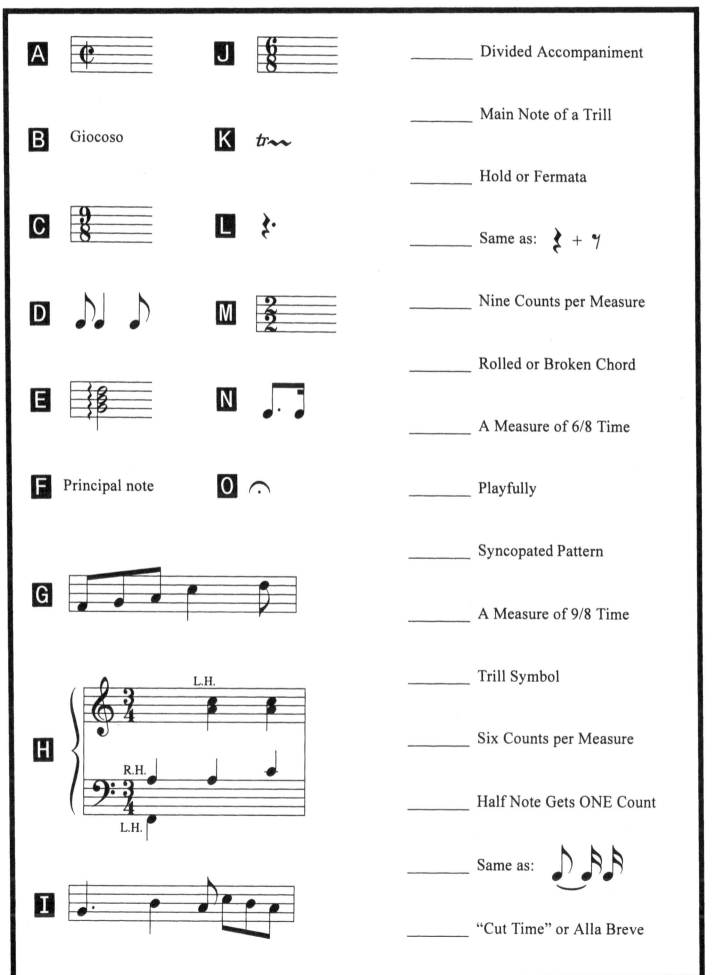

_____ Divided Accompaniment

_____ Main Note of a Trill

_____ Hold or Fermata

_____ Same as:

_____ Nine Counts per Measure

_____ Rolled or Broken Chord

_____ A Measure of 6/8 Time

_____ Playfully

_____ Syncopated Pattern

_____ A Measure of 9/8 Time

_____ Trill Symbol

_____ Six Counts per Measure

_____ Half Note Gets ONE Count

_____ Same as:

_____ "Cut Time" or Alla Breve